Tiger Woods

Additional Titles in the Sports Reports *Series*

Tiger Woods

Star Golfer

William W. Lace

Enslow Publishers, Inc.

40 Industrial Road	PO Box 38
Box 398	Aldershot
Berkeley Heights, NJ 07922	Hants GU12 6BP
USA	UK

http://www.enslow.com

Copyright © 1999 by William W. Lace

Library of Congress Cataloging-in-Publication Data

Lace, William W.
     Tiger Woods: star golfer / William W. Lace
        p. cm. —(Sports reports)
     Includes bibliographical references (p.) and index.
     Summary: A biography of the youngest golfer to win The
Masters Tournament, from his childhood in California to his
development as one of the most highly recognized players of
the game.
     ISBN 0-7660-1081-3
     1. Woods, Tiger—Juvenile literature. 2. Golfers—United
States—Biography—Juvenile literature. [1. Woods, Tiger.
2. Golfers. 3. Racially mixed people—Biography.]
I. Title II. Series.
GV964.W66L33   1999
796.352′092—dc21
[B]   98-36958
                                              CIP
                                              AC

Printed in the United States of America

10 9 8 7 6 5 4 3 2 1

To Our Readers:
All Internet addresses in this book were active and appropriate when we went to
press. Any comments or suggestions can be sent by e-mail to Comments@enslow.com
or to the address on the back cover.

Photo Credits: Courtesy Jerry W. Hoefer, pp. 6, 10, 13, 17, 23, 32, 34, 38, 48,
53, 62, 65, 74, 76, 78, 84, 89; Courtesy USGA / Robert Walker, pp. 42, 46.

Cover Photo: Courtesy Jerry W. Hoefer

Contents

Tiger Woods's talent on the golf course and winning smile have made him a favorite of fans all over the world.

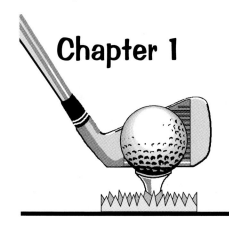

Chapter 1

The Youngest Master

Tiger Woods squatted low. He peered straight ahead through the tunnel formed by cupping his hands over the bill of his cap. Hundreds of golf fans watched him, ringing the thirteenth green at the Augusta National Golf Club on April 11, 1997. Woods did not see or hear them. His focus was on the white ball just in front of him and—twenty-five feet beyond the ball—the four-and-a-quarter-inch hole cut into the close-cut emerald grass.

Woods rose to his feet and took his stance to one side of the ball. He made two practice swings with his putter—nice, easy swings. The putt was down-hill, and he did not want to hit it too hard.

He stepped up to the ball, placing the blade of

his putter lightly on the ground behind it. One more glance at the hole, then a smooth, soft stroke. The ball rolled across the slanted green, curving a bit to the left. "Come on! Come on!" the crowd murmured.

Even before the ball reached the hole, Woods knew he had made the putt. He raised his putter into the air in anticipation. As the ball rattled into the cup, the crowd exploded with a great roar. Woods bowed his head briefly, and then looked up with a broad smile. He had made an eagle. More important, the twenty-one-year-old had just taken the lead in The Masters, one of the four most important golf tournaments in the world.

Two holes later, he added a birdie and finished the round in 66 strokes, six shots under the par of 72 for the Augusta National course. His total for two rounds was 136, eight under par. With two rounds to go, his nearest competitor, Colin Montgomerie of Scotland, was three shots back.

Woods and Montgomerie would play together the next day. People wondered whether Woods would feel the pressure of having the lead and being challenged by the thirty-three-year-old Montgomerie, one of the world's top golfers. "The pressure is mounting now, and I've got a lot more experience in major championship golf," Montgomerie told reporters.[1]

Anyone who thought of moving up on Tiger Woods was mistaken. Woods did most of the moving, and it was Montgomerie who seemed to wilt under the pressure.

On the second hole, a par-five, Woods hit his third shot only inches from the hole for a certain birdie. Montgomerie made a bogey on the hole, and Woods's lead was suddenly five shots. Tiger Woods then birdied the fifth hole with a twelve-foot putt and birdied the eighth hole while Montomerie took another bogey.

Woods finished with a seven-under-par 65 for the round. His three-round total of 201 was fifteen under par—a 54-hole Masters record. Montgomerie had shot a 78 and was twelve shots back. When asked what it would take to overtake Woods, he replied, "There is no chance. We're all human beings here, but there's no chance humanly possible that Tiger is just going to lose this tournament. No way. . . . Have you just come in or have you been away? Have you been on holiday or just arrived?"[2]

Other golfers were just as amazed by Tiger Woods's performance. "He's incredible," said Tom Watson. "He's a boy among men, but he's showing the men how to play golf at Augusta this year."[3] The

FACT

At a professional golf tournament, the players call Saturday "moving day." It is the day when everyone wants to shoot a low score to get in position for a victory in Sunday's final round.

The road to The Masters tournament brought not only a grueling schedule of tournaments and practice, but media attention as well. The news conferences at the tournaments became a chore that Tiger Woods sometimes found hard to deal with.

man in second place, Constanino Rocca, was asked whether he thought he could make up nine shots. "I think [it] is too many," the Italian said.[4]

It was, indeed, too many shots to make up. Wearing his trademark Sunday red shirt, Woods breezed through the final round of The Masters without a challenge. He made a bogey on hole 5—his first in thirty-seven holes—and another on hole 7 after hitting his drive left into a stand of trees. He more than made up for these mistakes, however, with five birdies.

The fans greeted Woods on each tee and each

green with standing ovations. On the sixteenth tee a group of young men bowed to him as they might to a monarch.

Just as Woods teed off on the eighteenth and final hole, a photographer snapped his picture. Woods jerked his drive far to the left, turned around, and glared at the photographer. "Please!" he said coldly.

Woods's second shot reached the green, about twenty-five feet from the hole. As he made his way through the crowd back to the eighteenth fairway, his mother, Kultida, and his father, Earl, applauded their son. The crowd also cheered. Even Rocca and his caddie stood to one side and applauded as Woods walked onto the eighteenth green.

Months later, Woods was asked what was going through his mind at that moment. "I saw everybody clapping and everything, but I looked at my putt and said, 'Geez, I've got a tough one.' My focus never left me."[5]

After Rocca putted out for a three-over-par 75, Woods knocked his first putt five feet past the hole. He studied the second putt carefully. If he made it, he would finish at 270, one shot better than the tournament record held by Jack Nicklaus and Raymond Floyd. After two practice strokes, he stepped up to the ball and tapped it gently. As it

FACT

The Augusta National course on which The Masters is played was designed by Robert "Bobby" Jones, one of the greatest golfers in history. Jones, who never played professionally, is the only player to have won the U.S. Open four times and the U.S. Amateur five times.

rolled into the hole, Woods swung his right fist in the air in celebration.

Tiger Woods had won The Masters! He shook Rocca's hand, embraced his caddie, Mike "Fluff" Cowan, then tearfully hugged his father. "Let it out," Earl Woods told his son. "Just let it all out."[6]

Not only had Woods broken the tournament record, but he also had won by more strokes—twelve—than any other player ever to win The Masters. It was the largest margin of victory in any of the major championships—The Masters, the United States Open, the British Open, and the Professional Golfers' Association (PGA) Championship—since 1862.

In the United States, golf is mostly a country club game played by upper-middle-class whites. It was not until 1961 that the PGA dropped the rule that "Caucasians only" could play in its tournaments.

Golf was exclusive, and The Masters, deep in the heart of Georgia, was the most exclusive tournament of all. Unlike most tournaments, The Masters was an invitation-only affair. African-American Charlie Sifford won PGA tournaments in 1967 and 1969 but did not get an invitation to The Masters. Only in 1975 did the tournament accept its first African-American player—Lee Elder.

Woods was well aware of what his victory

FACT

Tiger Woods—son of an African-American and American Indian father and a Thai, Chinese, and Dutch mother—was the first person of color ever to win a major golf championship.

Tiger Woods is shown with then-caddie, Mike "Fluff" Cowan.

meant, although he does not like racial labels. He calls himself a "Calblasian"—a mixture of Caucasian, black, American Indian, and Asian.

He said:

> Although I may be the first, I'm not a pioneer. Lee Elder, Charlie Sifford, Teddy Rhodes—those guys are the ones who paved the way for me to be here. . . . I was thinking about them and what they've done for me and the game of golf, and as I was coming up 18 I was having a little prayer of thanks to those guys.[7]

Elder had been in the crowd, cheering Woods all the way. "I think it certainly means a lot for minorities," he said later.

FACT

Although Tiger Woods, at age twenty-one, was the youngest player ever to win The Masters, he was not the youngest ever to win a major tournament. Thomas "Young Tom" Morris won the British Open in 1868 when he was nineteen, and Gene Sarazen won both the U.S. Open and the PGA Championship in 1922 at age twenty.

It's certainly going to be a situation where he's a role model. . . . One thing that has probably been keeping them [African Americans] back is that we did not have a champion like Tiger. I tried. Charlie [Sifford] tried. Jim Thorpe tried. But I think we were just a little bit before our time.[8]

Sifford had not made the trip to Augusta, but watched every minute on television from his home near Houston, Texas. He said:

For thirty-eight years I've been hoping something like this would happen. I got too old to be able to do it myself. But it's all over with now. Lee Elder played, and now Tiger has won it. I'm proud of them both.[9]

Woods's fellow professionals did not see his victory in terms of color. All they knew was that they had witnessed one of the greatest performers in the history of golf. "When I look at Tiger, I don't see color," said Paul Azinger. "I see the kid. And right now, the kid is the greatest golfer in the world."[10]

Jack Nicklaus, generally acknowledged to be the greatest golfer in history, agreed. "What he's done is establish himself as the heir apparent," he said. "He's got the whole world ahead of him. I don't think I want to go back and be 21 again and play against him."[11]

No one was prouder of Tiger Woods than his

father. Earl Woods was proud and happy, but he was not surprised. After all, he had been training his son for this moment since before the boy could walk. All those lessons, all those years of youth and amateur tournaments, had paid off—just as Earl Woods knew they would.

Earl Woods had predicted earlier in the week that his son would win The Masters. How did he know? "Because I had cleaned up everything that was a problem in his mind and that left the determining factor, talent," he said. "I'll take Tiger's chances with talent any day of the week with anybody on a golf course."[12]

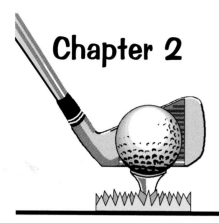

Chapter 2

Golf— A Brief Description

Golf is played on a large area of land called a course, on which there are eighteen holes. When all eighteen holes are played, this makes up a round. A hole consists of the tee, the area from which play is begun; the green, an area of very smooth, closely mown grass; and the fairway, the mown areas between the tee and the green. The grassy area on either side of the fairway is the rough.

On each green is a cylindrical hole, four and a quarter inches in diameter, called either the hole or the cup. Marking the hole is a small flag on a stick called the pin, or the flagstick. The object of golf is to hit the ball from the tee into the hole in as few strokes, or shots, as possible. The ball is struck with

Tiger Woods shows his usual excellent form as the ball flies through the air.

three kinds of clubs: woods are heavier and designed for long distances; irons are lighter and designed for shorter, more accurate shots; putters are used on the green to roll the ball toward the hole. Woods and irons come in various sizes and lofts, depending on the length of shot needed. The loft determines how high and far the ball will travel.

Par is the number of strokes a good golfer will require on a hole, and it depends on the distance to the hole from the tee. The par for most medium-length holes is four—one tee shot, one approach shot to the green, and two putts. Shorter holes are par-three; longer holes are par-five. Most golf courses have a total par of seventy to seventy-two strokes.

A score of one over par on a hole is a bogey. Two over par is a double-bogey, and so on. A score of one under par on a hole is a birdie. A score of two under par on a hole is an eagle.

Golf tournaments can be in two forms—match play and medal play (also known as stroke play). In medal play, the form used in most professional tournaments, the winner is the golfer who completes play—usually four rounds or seventy-two holes—in the fewest strokes.

In match play, which features two competitors, the winner is the golfer who wins the most number of holes. Total score does not count in match play,

FACT

The earliest written reference to golf was made in Scotland, where most experts think the sport began, more than five hundred years ago. In 1457, King James II passed a law banning golf and soccer because too much time was being spent playing those sports instead of training for military service by practicing archery.

and all eighteen holes do not have to be completed. For instance, if two golfers tie on the seventeenth hole and one of them is ahead by two holes (with no possibility of the other golfer catching up) the golfer who is ahead wins the match, 2–1, meaning that he or she is two ahead with only one hole remaining.

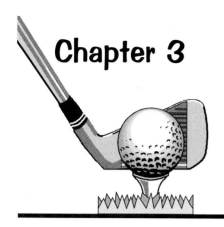

Chapter 3

The Cub

Earl Woods's Presbyterian upbringing taught him that everything is part of God's plan. He believes that he was put on earth and kept alive to be a guide to his son, Tiger. "The Almighty entrusted this precious child to me," he wrote. "He is orchestrating this entire scenario and has a plan to utilize Tiger to make an impact on the world. I don't know what it is, but I sincerely believe it will be spiritual and humanitarian and transcend the game of golf."[1]

If Earl Woods is correct, then Nguyen Phong, a lieutenant colonel in the South Vietnamese Army, was a big part of the plan, too. Twice during a mission in the Vietnamese jungle, Phong saved

Woods's life—once yelling out just before a sniper opened fire and then, only minutes later, warning the American that a poisonous snake was only inches from his face.

It was the late 1960s, and Woods, a lieutenant colonel in the U.S. Army Green Berets, was serving his second tour of duty in Vietnam. He and Phong were close friends. The South Vietnamese soldier was so fierce in combat that Woods began calling him Tiger. Woods, who was divorced and the father of one son, swore when he left Vietnam that if he ever had another son, he would be named Tiger.

Woods would meet another big part of the plan in Southeast Asia. While on an army assignment in Bangkok, Thailand, he met a secretary, Kultida Punsawad, and asked her for a date. She accepted, and in 1969 they were married.

Woods and Tida, as her friends call her, lived in Brooklyn, New York, after the war. It was there that Earl discovered golf. Even though he had never played the game, he agreed to a bet with a fellow officer.

Woods lost the golf bet, but vowed to get revenge. After four months of practice, he challenged the other officer and won by four shots. "I got hooked on golf in that round," he said. "I decided if I had another son, I'd introduce him to golf early on."[2]

FACT

Earl Woods came from an athletic background. He had played catcher on the baseball team at Kansas State University. As the only African-American player and the first in the entire Big Seven Conference, Woods had to endure racial taunts from opponents. Often, he could not stay in the same hotels or eat in the same restaurants as his teammates.

FACT

For years after the Vietnam War, Earl Woods tried to find and be reunited with Lieutenant Colonel Nguyen Phong, the man for whom Tiger Woods was named. In 1997, *Golf Digest* reporter Tom Callahan traveled to Vietnam and discovered that Phong had died on September 9, 1976, in a Communist prison camp. His widow was living in the United States, spoke very little English, and had never heard of Tiger Woods.

Shortly afterward, Woods retired from the Army and took a job as a purchaser for McDonald Douglas, an aircraft manufacturer in Southern California. Tida was expecting a baby, so she and Earl bought a small house in Cypress. They were the only people in the neighborhood who were not white. Their house was pelted with limes, and the windows were shot out with BB guns.

The former Green Beret refused to budge. So did his wife, who faced her neighbors with the calm of one raised as a Buddhist. Gradually, the vandalism ceased.

A few months later, on December 30, 1975, their son was born. Kultida made up a name for him—Eldrick—a combination of letters from her name and Earl's, starting with the first letter of Earl's name and ending with the first letter of her name. Earl didn't particularly like the name, but he didn't plan to use it anyway. He kept his promise to his wartime buddy and called his son Tiger.

Earl Woods continued to develop his golf game. In order to practice and keep an eye on young Tiger at the same time, he set up a net in his garage and hit golf balls into it from a carpet. Hour after hour he smacked balls into the net while his baby son watched from a high chair.

For months, little Tiger had been crawling

The covers for Woods's clubs were made by his mother, Kultida, and have the words "Love From Mom" in the language of her native Thailand.

around the house dragging his favorite toy, an old putter that Earl had shortened. One day, not yet ten months old, Tiger toddled over to the carpet while his dad was taking a break, put a ball down, gave the small club a little waggle, and—whack!—sent the ball into the net.

Earl ran into the house to find Tida. "We have a genius on our hands," he shouted.[3] Years later, when Tida attempted to throw the old high chair away, Earl stopped her. "You can't throw it away," he said. "That's going to be in the Hall of Fame some day."[4]

Tiger was now hooked on golf, too. He had other toys, but he mostly ignored them. He preferred to chase a tennis ball around the house, hitting it with a vacuum cleaner attachment.

When Tiger was eighteen months old, his father took him for the first time to the driving range at one of the nearby U.S. Navy golf courses. A few months later, he played his first hole, scoring an 11 on a 410-yard par-four.

Earl Woods knew by now that he and Tida did, indeed, have a genius—that Tiger could be to golf what Mozart was to music. Earl also knew he must be very careful not to push Tiger too far before he was ready. "The slightest miscalculation could have turned him against golf for the rest of his life," he wrote.[5]

When he was two, Tiger would call his father at work, practically begging to go practice later that afternoon. Earl would hesitate, keeping Tiger in suspense for a few seconds, before finally agreeing. "You see," Tiger later wrote of his father, "he never pushed me to play. Whether I practiced or played was always my idea."[6]

The practice began to pay off. Tiger won a pitch, putt, and drive contest at age three, competing against boys who were ten and eleven years old. He was scoring under 50 strokes for nine holes before he was four.

Not everyone was delighted with Tiger's abilities, however. The retired officers who played the Navy courses were not used to sharing the scene with an African American, much less a three-year-old. They began to enforce an old rule that children under ten could not play the course.

Tiger's mother soon found another place—Heartwell Golf Park, a course consisting of short, par-three holes. She asked the Heartwell professional (manager), Rudy Duran, if her four-year-old could play the course. Before he would agree, Duran wanted to see Tiger hit a few balls. "That was enough," Duran said later. "He had talent oozing out of his fingertips. He was a golfing genius with a natural swing and the ability to learn."[7]

FACT

Tiger first made the news at age three when a Los Angeles television station did a feature story on him. That led to his first appearance on national television, a putting contest against comedian Bob Hope on the *Merv Griffin Show*.

In addition to golf lessons, Tiger also received an unwelcome lesson in racism. On his first day of kindergarten in 1981, some older, white boys tied him to a tree, pelted him with rocks, and called him names. The boys were punished, but Tiger was now aware that some people would hate him simply because of the color of his skin.

At age five, Tiger got more national attention, appearing on the television show *That's Incredible*. "When I get big," he said, looking into the camera, "I'm going to beat Jack Nicklaus and Tom Watson."[8]

He was not able to beat Nicklaus and Watson just yet. In fact, when he was six, he played against a local professional and lost, even though he had led halfway through the round. He was bitterly disappointed. He walked off the eighteenth green in tears, not even stopping to shake hands with his opponent. That earned him a talking-to from his mother. "You must be a sportsman, win or lose," she lectured.[9]

Most of the job of disciplining Tiger fell to Tida. It was she who once asked officials in a junior tournament to penalize her son two strokes for throwing a club in anger. It was she who enforced the rule of no golf until homework was done. She never had trouble disciplining Tiger—all she had to do was take away his golf clubs.

From his father and Heartwell professional Rudy

Duran, Tiger learned the finer points of golf. He learned that hitting the ball a long way is not always what matters. He learned to hit the ball high or low, depending on how quickly he wanted it to stop. He learned to hit a fade, curving the ball to the right, or a draw, curving it to the left.

When he was only three, his father asked him what he had to think about before each shot. Tiger listed the distance needed, the "wawa" (water), the "sand twap" (trap), and how his ball sat on the ground. There was one more, Earl told him, hinting by blowing through his mouth. "Oh, the wind, Daddy, the wind," exclaimed Tiger.[10]

Tiger also learned patience. When he would bang his club on the ground after a bad shot, his father would calmly ask, "Whose responsibility was that bad shot?" After thinking it over, Tiger would reply, "Mine."[11]

He learned self-reliance. Once, after they arrived at Heartwell, Tiger asked his father whether he had put his clubs in the trunk of the car. He was told that his clubs were his own responsibility. While Earl practiced by himself, Tiger fought to keep from crying. Finally, Earl produced the clubs. He had hidden them after he knew Tiger had forgotten them. Tiger was happy to be able to play, but he had also learned his lesson.

When Tiger was six, Earl began his mental training. He bought tape recordings containing subliminal messages—words spoken so softly they could barely be heard but that in time, become imbedded in the mind. Tiger not only listened; he wrote the phrases down and tacked them to the walls of his bedroom where he could see them every day:

I believe in me.
I focus and give it my all.
I do it all with my heart.

That same year—1982—Tiger entered his first national competition, the Optimist Junior World Tournament in San Diego, California. He stepped up to the first tee and hit his drive long and straight. His father later asked him what was going on in his mind as he started his first big tournament. "Where I wanted the ball to go, Daddy," he answered.[12]

Tiger Woods was ready for competitive golf. He did not win that first tournament, but he finished eighth of 150 golfers, and all seven players ahead of him were four years older than he was. The world of golf was starting to see a new star on the horizon.

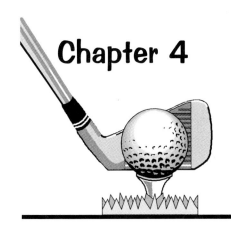

Chapter 4

Child Prodigy

In 1985, when Tiger Woods was nine years old, his mother took him to Thailand to introduce him to that part of his cultural background. While they were in Bangkok, she showed a chart she had kept on Tiger according to a Thai Buddhist ritual to a monk.

"He said Tiger [is] going to be [a] leader. If he [goes] in the Army, he [will] be a four-star general," she reported later. "The monk [didn't] know about golf. Monks don't watch TV. The monk said it's like God [sent an] angel."[1]

Tiger was, indeed, something special on a golf course. Those who had to play against him, however, probably did not exactly regard him as an angel.

For years, he had been regularly winning local American Junior Golf Association tournaments. In 1984, at the age of eight, he began beating older boys from all over the country. He won the Optimist Junior World under-ten division that year and the next. He would eventually win six Junior World championships in various age groups. No other golfer had ever won more than three.

In 1986, Tiger's father decided that he needed a more experienced teacher and placed him under the guidance of John Anselmo of the Meadowlark Golf Club in Huntingdon Beach. "I saw so much rhythm and balance, even when he was 10," Anselmo said. "I was awed by it. I knew even at that time he was special."[2]

There was never a doubt in Tiger's mind that he would become a professional golfer—and a good one. He posted a chart on his bedroom wall. It showed how old the great Jack Nicklaus had been when he accomplished various feats—first round under 70 strokes, first U.S. Amateur Championship, first championship in a major tournament—and left spaces for him to put his own age when he did the same thing. "Nicklaus was my hero," he said later, "and I thought it would be great to accomplish all the things he did even earlier than he accomplished them."[3]

As Tiger set his sights higher and higher, Earl Woods knew that a different kind of lesson needed to be learned. Physical ability was only one part of what it took to play at the highest levels. The world-class golfer must be mentally strong, as well—able to ignore distractions even when they come deliberately from an opponent. While Anselmo worked on Tiger's swing, Earl worked on his concentration.

"I taught him every little trick that an opponent could possibly pull on him in match play, and some that I invented myself," Earl said. "It was a very difficult thing to do, and it didn't fill me with pride and joy. But if he was going to continue in golf, I felt it was necessary."[4]

Just as Tiger was about to swing, for instance, his father would cough, jingle coins in his pocket, or rip the Velcro on his golf glove. On the green, Earl would stand where Tiger could see him and then move just as Tiger was starting to putt. He cheated deliberately and made sure Tiger knew he was cheating.

Tiger knew what Earl was trying to teach him, but he still grew angry. He would turn around and glare at his father, who would say, "Don't look at me. Are you going to hit the ball or not?"[5]

Eventually, Tiger developed what Earl called a "coldness." Nothing his father could do disturbed

Tiger Woods's concentration is reflected in his face as he follows the flight of a tee shot.

his focus. "I wanted to make sure he'd never run into anybody who was tougher mentally than he was," Earl said.[6]

Another member of what was now being called "Team Tiger" was Jay Brunza, a clinical psychologist and former Navy captain with whom Earl had played golf. Brunza had worked with athletes at the U.S. Naval Academy, helping them sharpen their mental approach to sports. At Earl's request he began working with Tiger.

He paid his first visit to the Woods's home when Tiger was thirteen. He taught him some techniques that would help him to focus even harder as he played. The next day, Brunza and Tiger joined a group for a round at the Navy course. After the first seven holes, Tiger was five under par. One of Brunza's friends asked the psychologist, "What kind of monster have you created?"[7]

Brunza next began to hypnotize Tiger, planting ideas and concepts deep in his mind that would help him respond positively under pressure and channel any anger or frustration following a bad shot into a determination to do better. "I like the feeling of trying my hardest under pressure," Tiger would say later. "But it's so intense, it's hard to describe. It feels like a lion is tearing at my heart."[8]

By this time, Earl had retired from his job (at age fifty-six) and began to devote himself entirely to Tiger, taking his son to tournaments all over the country. In August 1989, they went to Texarkana, Arkansas, for the Insurance Youth Golf Classic, also known as the Big I. In the final round of the tournament, professional golfers played alongside the youngsters. Tiger was paired with John Daly, who would later go on to win both PGA Championship and British Open titles.

The six-foot, muscular Daly was famous for his

Tiger Woods uses his hands to create "tunnel vision" to block out everything except the putt he is studying.

long drives. On this day, however, he was being matched shot for shot by a junior high school student who stood 5 feet 5 inches and weighed 107 pounds. After nine holes, Tiger was two strokes under par and Daly was one over. "I can't let this 13-year-old beat me," Daly told a friend.[9]

Daly was able to avoid embarrassment, making birdies on three of the last four holes to beat Tiger by two strokes. Tiger's score of 72, however, was still good enough to beat eight of the professionals who played that day.

Tiger finished the tournament in second place behind seventeen-year-old Justin Leonard, another future star. Leonard said, "It's spectacular that he's that young and is able to play on this level."[10]

The next year, Tiger did even better. He became the youngest player ever to win the Big I, shooting a 69 in the final round. That was better than eighteen of the twenty-one professionals, including Tommy Moore, who played with Tiger. "I wish I could have played like that at 14," Moore said. "Heck, I wish I could play like that at 27."[11]

In the fall of 1990, Tiger entered high school. Although golf took up most of his time, he tried other sports, as well. He was good at both baseball and track but eventually gave them up to devote more time to golf.

He had some time for girls, but not much. He began to grow taller but remained thin, even though his diet—when he had a choice—consisted mostly of cheeseburgers, tacos, and pizza. His grades were excellent—mostly As with a sprinkling of Bs. "I'm just a normal kid who happens to play golf pretty well," he told one reporter.[12]

Tiger was playing golf better than just pretty well. He had always made it a practice not to try to move up to the next level before he felt he was ready. In February 1991, however, he felt prepared for a big leap forward. He attempted to become the youngest player ever to qualify for a professional tournament.

He was one of 132 golfers, almost all of them professionals, playing at the Los Cerranos Country Club in Chino, California. Only the two best scorers would make it into the Nissan Los Angeles Open the following week.

The way Tiger was playing, it looked as if he might be one of the two lucky ones. He birdied the sixteenth hole after unleashing a monster drive of 344 yards. Then he made birdie on seventeen to go six under par. Mac O'Grady had already posted a score of eight under par. Tiger thought he had to have an eagle three on the par-five eighteenth to make it.

His drive on eighteen came to rest on a bare spot in the fairway. To make things worse, the ball was on a downhill slope. It would be almost impossible, from this position, to hit the ball the remaining 250 yards to the green. Tiger tried it anyway, but the ball splashed into a pond short of the green. He made a bogey six and wound up with a 69, three shots behind O'Grady and John Burckle.

Tiger hadn't made it into the Los Angeles Open, but he was the talk of the tournament, anyway. One of his playing partners, Ron Hinds, said, "You try to avoid envy in golf, but that kid humbled us all."[13]

In April 1991, one of Tiger's dreams came true—a meeting with Jack Nicklaus. Nicklaus was being honored at the annual Friends of Golf charity tournament at the Bel Air Country Club in Los Angeles. Tiger was invited to appear with him at a golf clinic, an exhibition.

Nicklaus, winner of more major golf championships than any other player, had heard about Tiger. He had been impressed by what he had heard. He was even more impressed by what he saw. "When I grow up," the Golden Bear told the Tiger, "I hope my swing is as pretty as yours."[14]

That summer, Tiger established himself as the top junior golfer in the country. He won the Optimist International Junior World Tournament for

FACT

The normally self-confident Tiger Woods was quiet and shy when he was introduced to Jack Nicklaus and to the crowd sprinkled with Hollywood personalities. However, his nervousness disappeared, when he stepped up to the tee and began booming long drives.

Woods's long arms and wide shoulders allow him to generate tremendous club speed, so he can hit longer than most golfers.

the sixth time. He won the Los Angeles City Junior Championship and the Southern California Championship. This was not bad for a fifteen-year-old, but the real accomplishments—the ones that would begin making Tiger Woods a legend—were just around the corner.

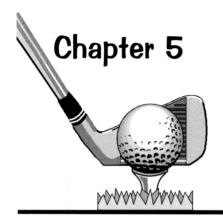

Chapter 5

The Legend Grows

At the age of fifteen, Tiger Woods had won just about everything junior golf had to offer. The exception, however, was the biggest tournament of all—the United States Junior Amateur Championship, or Junior Am.

The Junior Am—open to boys under eighteen—and the U.S. Amateur—open to male amateurs of any age—are hard, weeklong combinations of stroke play and match play. First, the field of 312 golfers who have qualified play thirty-six holes. The top sixty-four then advance to match play. The eventual winner thus has to make it into the top sixty-four and then survive six head-to-head matches.

The 1991 Junior Am was at the Bay Hill Club in

Orlando, Florida. Tiger came into the tournament with experience, having reached the semifinals the year before. He had also played Bay Hill the previous summer and was familiar with the course. He led the stroke play at 140, four under par, and easily dispatched his first five opponents in match play.

The final against Brad Zwetschke was a different story. Tiger quickly went ahead by three holes, but he faltered on the back nine and bogeyed eighteen to even the match and go into a playoff. On the first hole of the playoff, Tiger had a bogey, but it was good enough. Zwetschke took a double-bogey, and Tiger was the champion—the youngest in the forty-five-year history of the event.

It took a while for the importance of his victory to sink in. "The pressure is so awesome, and I was so tired, I couldn't talk afterward," he said later.[1] On the plane back to California, however, he asked his father if he could look at the medal he had won. Moments later, when Earl turned to look at him, tears were streaming down Tiger's face.

The Junior Am championship qualified Tiger for his first U.S. Amateur, where he would face the best nonprofessional golfers in the country. He missed the top sixty-four but gained valuable experience.

In March 1992, Tiger played in his first PGA Tour event, accepting an invitation from the Los Angeles

FACT

The Junior Am is one of several national championships to be sponsored annually by the United States Golf Association (USGA), the official ruling body of golf in America. Of all the tournaments in the world, only the British Open carries as much prestige as do USGA championships.

At age fifteen, Tiger Woods became the youngest winner of the Junior Amateur Championship.

Open to play as an amateur. Some of the best professionals in the world were there, but Tiger was the center of media attention. On the first tee, he said he was "so tense I had a tough time holding the club."[2] Nevertheless, he made a birdie on the hole—a great start in his first-ever PGA Tour event.

He shot a 72 in the first round but slipped to a 75 on Friday and missed the cut—the score necessary to qualify for the final two rounds. Still, similar to the U.S. Amateur, it was a learning experience, and Tiger said, "I learned that I'm not that good."[3]

The 1992 Junior Amateur at the Wollaston (Massachusetts) Golf Club was almost a repeat of the year before. Tiger Woods won the medal play part of the tournament at 143 and then swept through to the final. Again, he had a tough match. His opponent, Mark Wilson, was two holes ahead with only six to play. Tiger, however, showed his usual ability to turn his game up a notch in the clutch. He birdied holes 14, 16, and 18 to win by one hole—the only person ever to win two Junior Ams.

Again, he had qualified for the U.S. Amateur, held that year at Dublin, Ohio's, Muirfield Village Golf Club—home course of Jack Nicklaus. Tiger lost his composure midway through the first round of stroke play, scoring a quadruple-bogey seven on the eleventh hole and finishing with a 78. He stormed off the course, furious at himself, but returned the next day to shoot a 66 and qualify for match play. When reporters asked what had calmed him down, Tiger replied, "Dinner. I had 10 tacos and that was it."[4]

Tiger won his first match, beating Ted Gleason, a twenty-two-year-old college senior, but then ran into hot-shooting Tim Herron, and lost in

FACT

The most successful young golfers have not necessarily gone on to outstanding careers. Of the twenty-three winners of the U.S. Junior Amateur, Tiger Woods was only the third to later win one of golf's major tournaments. The others were Gay Brewster (1967 Masters) and Johnny Miller (1973 U.S. Open and 1976 British Open.)

fourteen holes. (Herron later became a professional.) Tiger always knew when he was in over his head. "My game's not fine-tuned enough for this yet," he said. "The swing's not there yet."[5]

By now, Tiger was the best-known young player in the country. More PGA Tour tournaments wanted him to play, knowing that his presence would help sell tickets. In the spring of 1993, now seventeen years old, he played in the Los Angeles Open, the Honda Classic, and the GTE Byron Nelson Classic. He was getting a taste of the pro golf tour, and it tasted good. "Daddy," he told Earl at the Honda Classic, "I could get used to this very easy."[6]

Tiger's third Junior Am turned out to be his toughest. He had just recovered from mononucleosis—an illness that left him constantly tired—and was feeling weak. He failed to lead the stroke play, finishing three shots behind fellow Californian Ted Oh. When match play started, however, he seemed like the old Tiger, easily beating five opponents—including Oh—to reach the final against Ryan Armour.

Tiger had defeated Armour handily the year before at Wollaston (in the 1992 Junior Am), but this year it was different. After losing the sixteenth hole, Woods was dormie, meaning he had to win all the remaining holes just to tie. As he had the previous year, he shifted his game into high gear. He sank an eight-foot putt on the seventeenth hole for a birdie. Then he birdied on the eighteenth to send the match into a playoff, which he won with a par on the first hole.

"It was the most amazing comeback of my career," he said afterward. "I had to play the two best holes of my life under the toughest circumstances, and I did it."[7]

In the summer of 1993, Tiger again tried his luck in the U.S. Amateur. Again, he lost in the second round of match play. The week wasn't a total loss, however. He met Butch Harmon. Harmon was head professional at Houston's Lochinvar Golf Club. He had worked with some of the game's best, including Davis Love III, Steve Elkington, and one of Tiger's boyhood heroes—Greg Norman.

Both Tiger and his father had been thinking that John Anselmo had taken Tiger as far as he could. His game was close to being as good as that of a pro, so he needed a pro's pro.

Harmon agreed to take on Tiger Woods as a student. He made slight alterations in his swing and began to teach him how to better control the distances on his shots. "He was this skinny kid with this long, loose golf swing with absolutely no control over where the ball was going," Harmon

Tiger Woods usually knew when his game was fine-tuned enough to meet the next challenge of his career.

said. "He hit it as hard as he could, found it, and hit it again."[8]

Harmon's work began to show results. Tiger Woods was almost unbeatable in 1993–94, his senior year of high school. He even made his first cut in a professional tournament—the Johnnie Walker Asian Classic in Thailand, his mother's homeland. He was more than ready when time came for the 1994 U.S. Amateur at the Tournament Players Club–Sawgrass course in Ponte Vedra, Florida.

Woods easily qualified for match play, shooting 65–72–137. He disposed of his first two opponents, and then came from three holes down with six to play to beat University of Florida golf coach Buddy Alexander. Two more victories put him into the final against his good friend Trip Kuehne, a senior at Oklahoma State University.

Kuehne was hot from the start. He birdied seven of the first thirteen holes, to go six holes up. Fortunately for Tiger, the final of the U.S. Amateur is played over thirty-six holes. After the first eighteen, still four holes down, Woods said, "How's that for a whipping? He put a number on me."[9] Earl Woods was not worried. "Let the legend grow," he whispered to his son.[10]

In the afternoon round, Woods clawed his way back. He birdied the sixteenth to pull even. Then

FACT

Tiger Woods and Trip Kuehne's sister, Kelli, are about the same age and know each other from junior golf. Woods and his father once stayed with the Kuehnes in Texas when Tiger played a junior tournament.

came the seventeenth, a frightening par-three with a green almost entirely surrounded by water. The hole was on the back right of the green, only a few yards from the water. The safe play would have been to the middle of the green, but Woods was not playing it safe. His pitching wedge hit on the back of the green, took one hop, then spun back only three feet from the water's edge.

Back home in California, Woods's mother fell off her bed as she watched the shot on television. "That

Tiger Woods acknowledges the applause of the gallery after sinking a birdie putt.

boy almost gave me a heart attack," she said later. "All I kept saying was, 'God, don't let that ball go in the water.'"[11]

Woods then sank the fourteen-foot putt for birdie to win the hole. He leaped in the air and pumped his fist in triumph. On the final hole, Kuehne's bogey gave Tiger the victory. At eighteen, Tiger Woods had become the youngest champion in the ninety-four-year history of the U.S. Amateur and the first of African-American ancestry. "Son," his father told him, "you have done something no black person in the United States has ever done, and you will forever be a part of history."[12]

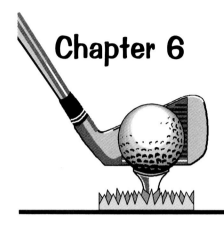

Chapter 6

Student and Superstar

In the summer of 1994, Tiger Woods made the transition from the top of junior golf to the top of amateur golf look easy. That fall, he would face another important transition—from high school to college.

Tiger Woods had long been getting letters from golf coaches urging him to consider their colleges. No coach, however, had been pursuing Woods longer than Stanford University's Wally Goodwin, who had first written in 1989. When the time came, Woods chose Stanford because of its superior academic reputation. "School has always come first," he said, "and that meant Stanford."[1]

By winning the U.S. Amateur, Tiger Woods had

become a national celebrity. When he entered Stanford in the fall, however, he considered himself just another student in a university where almost all the students are exceptional. "When I was in high school, I set the curve," he said. "Here, I follow it."[2]

As a freshman on a golf team loaded with seniors, he was stuck with the rollaway bed in hotel rooms. He had to carry the luggage of the older players.

On the golf course, however, Woods was not just another freshman. He won his first college tournament even before classes started, shooting a four-under-par 68 to win the Tucker Invitational in Albuquerque, New Mexico, by three shots.

Tiger Woods had a lot more on his plate than college golf, however. By winning the U.S. Amateur, he had earned a spot in The Masters in April 1995. It would be the first time for him to play any of the four major tournaments, and he wanted to be ready. To prepare himself for the lightning-fast Augusta National greens, Woods practiced putting on the hardwood basketball floor in the Maples Pavilion Stanford Basketball Arena.

When Tiger Woods arrived at Augusta National in April 1995, he was impressed but not overwhelmed. "The average golfer that goes there is blown away with Magnolia Lane [the avenue

FACT

Stanford senior Notah Begay, after seeing Tiger Woods in the thick glasses he wore when he was not wearing contact lenses, started calling him Urkel after the character in the television show *Family Matters*.

leading to the clubhouse] and the history and tradition of The Masters," Earl Woods said. "That doesn't impress the black golfer [because of past discrimination]."[3]

Tiger Woods soon found that the greens were as slick as advertised. His first putt, a thirty-footer, went past the hole, off the green, and down a hill. It came to rest fifty feet from the hole. He made a bogey on the hole but recovered with a birdie on the second hole and went on to shoot an even-par 72—four shots better than Jack Nicklaus in his Masters debut. He shot another 72 on Friday and thus made the cut. This was the first time he had made the cut in the United States.

After the round, Tiger Woods and his father went to a nearby city-owned course where Tiger gave a clinic for African-American young people. In the crowd were many men who had caddied at The Masters when the only blacks allowed on the course were those who carried golf bags for the whites. "We are acknowledging that we know who came before Tiger and that they suffered humiliation, and that we realize the debt. It's a way of saying thank you and a promise to carry the baton," his father said.[4]

A 77 on Saturday took Woods out of the running, but he came back with another 72 on Sunday and

FACT

The Masters was the last golf tournament to admit African-American players. Augusta National did not have an African-American member until 1990.

Wherever Tiger Woods plays, the crowd is sure to include young fans.

finished tied for forty-first at five over par. Before he left to return to Stanford, he gazed over the framed pictures of former Masters champions displayed on a wall. "Someday, I'm going to get my picture up there," he said.[5]

By that July, when Woods arrived in Newport, Rhode Island, for the U.S. Amateur, he had had a lackluster early summer. He had finished fifth in the National Collegiate Athletic Association (NCAA) tournament. He dropped out of his first-ever U.S. Open with a wrist injury and finished sixty-eighth in his first British Open.

He wanted to become the ninth player in history to win back-to-back Amateurs, but he almost did not survive stroke play, shooting a 68 and a 74. Once match play started, however, he was back in a groove. His work with Butch Harmon was paying off. He was never behind through his first five matches.

In the final, Tiger Woods faced forty-three-year-old Buddy Marucci. Woods fell three holes back in the early going but was only one down after the first eighteen. In the afternoon, Woods grabbed the lead on the twenty-fourth hole of the match. Marucci refused to crumble, however, and was only one down going into the final hole.

Marucci's second shot to the eighteenth green

left him with a tough, twenty-three-foot downhill putt. Woods had 140 yards to the hole. He knew if he hit his normal 8 iron, the ball would fly too far. He tried what he and Harmon had been working on—a "knock-down" shot on which Woods shortened his swing to reduce the distance. The ball hit fourteen feet beyond the hole and—thanks to the backspin Woods had put on it—drew back to within eighteen inches of the hole to clinch the victory.

Tiger Woods knew he was a much better golfer than he had been when he won his first Amateur. "This one means more because it shows how far my game has come," he said. "That shot at 18. That's the only shot I could hit close, that half-shot. I didn't have it last year and I didn't have it at Augusta."[6]

Ever since he had won his first Amateur, the golf world had been wondering when he would turn professional. The fans wanted to know. The media wanted to know. Even his Stanford teammates could not help asking him. "He would always give you sort of an indecisive answer," said Eric Crum, a Stanford classmate. "He always sort of avoided the question."[7]

Woods and his parents had always said that Tiger would get his college degree before turning pro. Two incidents during 1995 began to change their minds. First, he was suspended briefly by the

FACT

Tiger Woods's victory in the 1996 U.S. Amateur gave him six United States Golf Association titles—three U.S. Amateurs and three U.S. Junior Amateurs. Only four golfers have ever won more USGA championships. Bobby Jones won nine, all as an amateur; Jack Nicklaus and JoAnne Gunderson Carner won eight each; and Ann Quast Sander won seven. Hollis Stacy and Glenna Collett Vare have six victories along with Tiger Woods.

FACT

When Tiger Woods thought he might be penalized by the National Collegiate Athletic Association (NCAA) for allowing Arnold Palmer to buy him dinner, he sent Palmer a check for twenty-five dollars. Woods later donated the canceled check to a charity auction, where it sold for five thousand dollars.

NCAA for having written a diary of his Masters experience for a golf magazine, even though he had not been paid. Then, in October, he arranged to have dinner with Arnold Palmer. He wanted to ask the golf legend how he had handled all the pressure, all the publicity. They ate at a restaurant, and Palmer paid the bill.

Stanford officials, afraid Tiger had broken an NCAA rule on accepting gifts, suspended him for one day. He began to wonder whether he wanted to endure such minor hassling for two more years. He backed away from earlier statements, giving himself more options. "If I get to where I can't learn anything more from playing college golf, or if I get burned out like I did playing junior golf, I might turn pro," he said.[8]

Woods's decision would be based on his performance in five 1996 tournaments—The Masters, the NCAA Championships, the U.S. Open, the British Open, and the U.S. Amateur. He would take particular aim at the NCAA and the U.S. Amateur. If he won those, there would be little else for him to accomplish as an amateur.

The year got off to a rocky start when he shot 75–75 and missed the cut at The Masters. Woods was disappointed but thought his game had shown some improvement. "I know exactly what I have to work on," he said.[9]

He must have worked hard. At the NCAA Championships at Ooltehwah, Tennessee, he was eleven under par through the first three rounds, including a course-record 67 in the second round. Even though he shot an 80 on the final day, he won the championship by four strokes.

The U.S. Open, played at Oakland Hills in Michigan, was another disappointment. Woods made the cut, but his fourteen-over-par score left him tied for eighty-second.

The breakthrough came in the British Open, played at Royal Lytham in England in August. Once again Woods started slowly, shooting a 75 on opening day. In the second round, however, he was seven under par over the last thirteen holes for a 66—the lowest score ever by an amateur. "Something really clicked that day," he said later. "Ever since, the game has seemed a lot easier."[10]

He finished with two rounds of 70 and tied for twenty-second, receiving the silver medal as low amateur. It was nice, he said, but "Heck, I was looking for the Claret Jug [the British Open championship trophy]. That's what I came here for."[11]

Later that month, Tiger Woods set out to become

the first man to win three straight U.S. Amateurs. Reporters were predicting that if he won, he would turn professional. Woods was not talking. He told everyone, including his coach, that he would be back at Stanford in the fall.

Tiger Woods led stroke play with rounds of 69 and 67 over the Pumpkin Ridge course in Cornelius, Oregon. He did not have any tough opposition in match play until the semifinal, when he came from two holes down to beat Stanford teammate Joel Kribel.

In the final, he faced Steve Scott, a University of Florida sophomore. Their match proved to be one of the most exciting ever. Woods's game was off during the morning round, and Scott's was on. Scott led after the first round by five holes, but he knew how Woods could come back. ". . . I won't be happy until I have him 10 up or something," he said. "He's that tough."[12]

Indeed, he was. Nine holes deep into the afternoon, Scott's lead had shrunk to one. He fought back, however, and was two up with only three holes left.

It was time, once again, for Tiger Woods to put his game in high gear, and that is exactly what he did. He birdied the sixteenth hole, the thirty-third hole of the match, to cut Scott's lead to one. Then, on seventeen, he sank a difficult, thirty-foot putt to draw even. It was an incredible putt, especially under such pressure. "That's a feeling I'll remember for the rest of my life," said Woods.[13]

Both players parred the final hole to send the match into overtime. Both made pars on the first extra hole, but on the second, a par-three, Scott drove in the rough. Woods's ball was only seven feet away from the hole. Scott chipped to within six feet but missed his par putt. Woods sank his par putt of eighteen inches, and the title was his.

Tiger Woods had accomplished everything he could in amateur golf, but when reporters asked him after his victory whether he would now turn pro, he said he had not made up his mind. Actually, he had. Later than night he told his parents, "Yep, it's time to go."[14]

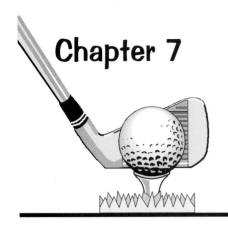

Chapter 7

Professional Golfer

On Tuesday, August 27, 1996, just two days after his victory in the U.S. Amateur, Tiger Woods made it official. He declared himself a professional. The next day, one day before the start of the Greater Milwaukee Open, he began a news conference by saying, "I guess, Hello, world."[1]

All the plans had been made. For six years, International Management Group (IMG), agents for many sports stars, had been eyeing Tiger Woods as a potential client. In 1990, Hughes Norton, of IMG's golf division, had talked with Earl Woods. "The first black superstar on the tour is going to make himself and somebody else a whole lot of money," Earl told

Norton. "That's why we're here, Mr. Woods," Norton answered.[2]

In Milwaukee, it was announced that Tiger Woods had signed with IMG. Furthermore, Norton told reporters, Woods had signed a blockbuster deal with the Nike sportswear company—$40 million over five years.

Some people thought Nike had paid too much. The head of Nike, Phil Knight, thought otherwise. "What Michael Jordan did for basketball, [Tiger Woods] absolutely can do for golf," he said. "The world has not seen anything like what he's going to do for the sport."[3]

In addition to the Nike deal, Woods signed another with Titleist, a golf equipment company, for $20 million. That kind of money was enough to create jealously in some of his fellow professionals. "Here's a guy who hasn't even gotten his [PGA] Tour card yet and he's making $60 million," said Steve Stricker.[4]

Indeed, Tiger Woods still had to earn the right to become a regular member of the PGA Tour. To do so, he would have to finish among the top 125 money winners in 1996 or win a PGA event. If he did neither, he would have to be among the top players at the PGA Tour's qualifying tournament in December. There were only a few tournaments left

FACT

When Tiger Woods won both the U.S. Amateur Championship and the NCAA Championship in 1996, he became only the third golfer to win both titles in the same year. The others to do so were Jack Nicklaus in 1961 and Phil Mickelsen in 1990.

The trademark "swoosh" on Tiger Woods's clothing reflect his $40 million deal with the Nike sportswear company.

on the 1996 PGA Tour schedule, but seven of them had offered Tiger Woods a sponsor's exemption. The exemption would allow him to play even if he was not an official Tour member.

Milwaukee was the first. Decked out in new clothes covered with the Nike symbol, Tiger Woods birdied three of his first five holes and shot a four-under-par 67. He followed that on Friday with a 69, but his two-round total was eight shots behind the leader. "Geez," he said, "what do you have to do out here?"[5]

With Woods for the first time was a new caddie, Mike "Fluff" Cowan. His nickname came from his drooping white mustache. Woods had borrowed Cowan from his regular pro, Peter Jacobsen, who was out with an injury. Four weeks later, Cowan became a fixture of Team Tiger. Said Woods at that time, "Fluff is not only a caddie for me, he's also one of my best friends. Fluff has the guts to speak up down the stretch . . . and I value his opinion. (In March 1999 Mike "Fluff" Cowan and Tiger Woods came to a parting of the ways.)"[6]

Tiger Woods slipped to a 73 on Saturday and recovered with a final-round 68, but that left him in a tie for sixtieth place. His winnings for the week came to $2,544. Not much next to his Nike deal, but it was huge to Tiger. "The money I make on the golf course—now that's done through blood, sweat and tears," he said. "I am not saying the contracts are bad. But I am more satisfied by the money I earn playing. That $2,544 I earned at Milwaukee will go down in history for me."[7]

The next stop after Milwaukee was the Canadian Open. Tiger Woods was tired, but he had a chance to rest when rain wiped out the third round. Refreshed, he shot a 68 on Sunday—the best round of the day—and finished in a tie for eleventh, winning $37,500.

Next was the Quad Cities Classic in Coal Valley, Illinois, a tournament normally bypassed by the better-known players. With Tiger Woods in the field, all attendance records were broken. An extra fifteen thousand tickets were printed—and even that was not nearly enough.

Woods shot a first-round 69 on Thursday and followed on Friday with a 64 to take a one-shot lead. He kept the lead with another 69 on Saturday. Some of the top golf reporters rushed to Illinois from Washington, D.C., where they had been covering the prestigious President's Cup. Everybody wanted to be there when Tiger Woods won his first PGA event.

That win would not come this week, however. On the fourth hole Sunday, Tiger hooked his drive into a pond, then hit a tree. He wound up with a quadruple-bogey eight. Later, he took four putts on

Tiger Woods learned early in his career as a pro golfer that it is important to maintain one's cool and act as a true professional.

FACT

In 1996, Tiger Woods did not play the minimum 50 rounds to be ranked in the PGA Tour's statistical categories. His totals for the 41 rounds he played would have ranked him first in average driving distance (288.8 yards) and birdies per round (4.2), second in average score per round (69.32), and fourth in the number of greens reached in the regulation amount of strokes (71.7 percent).

the seventeenth green and dropped to a tie for fifth. Tiger was disappointed but philosophical. "The way I look at it," he said, "is that I broke in at Milwaukee and did okay. I did better in Canada. Today I not only broke the top ten barrier, but the top five, too. So that's progress."[8]

He made even more progress the next week, finishing third in the B.C. Open in Endicott, New York. His $58,000 paycheck ran his total to $140,194—good enough for one hundred twenty-eighth on the money list after only four tournaments.

The following week was the Buick Challenge in Pine Mountain, Georgia. Not only was Tiger Woods the main attraction, but a special dinner was planned for him on Thursday night. He would receive the Fred Haskins Award as the top college player of the year. Woods, however, was worn out, having played twenty-three rounds of competitive golf over the last thirty-five days. To the dismay of the tournament sponsors and Buick, which had spent thirty thousand dollars on the award dinner, he pulled out. While Hughes Norton gave the sponsors the bad news, Woods was flying to Orlando, Florida, where he was now living.

Tiger Woods came under immediate criticism, not only from the media, but also from his fellow professionals. Arnold Palmer and Jack Nicklaus, they said, would never have pulled out like this. "Everybody's been telling him how great he is," said Davis Love III. "I guess he's starting to believe it."[9]

Woods knew he had made a terrible mistake. Weeks later, speaking at the rescheduled award dinner, he said, "I should've attended the dinner. I admit I was wrong . . . but I learned from that, and I will never make that mistake again."[10]

Most of his fellow golfers were willing to forget the incident. They realized Woods still had some growing up to do. "I'd hate to have the press covering all my screw ups when I was 20 years old," said Butch Harmon, Woods's coach.[11]

Tiger Woods's date with destiny finally came the next week at the Las Vegas Invitational. He started slowly—as usual—with a first-day 70, putting him in eighty-third place. Fortunately for him, this tournament was played over five rounds instead of the usual four. He battled back with a nine-under-par 63 on Thursday and followed the next two days with a 68 and a 67, four shots off the lead.

The next day was Sunday, October 6, 1996. "This could be the day," said Harmon. "His swing looked really good on the practice range."[12] It was, indeed, Woods's day. He birdied four holes on the back nine for a 64. He was twenty-eight under par for ninety holes, but he was not through yet. Davis Love III, playing several groups behind Tiger, posted the same total, forcing a sudden-death playoff. The first player to win a hole would win the tournament.

Both players drove down the middle of the fairway on the first playoff hole. Woods then hit his second shot onto the green, seven feet away from the hole. Love's second shot landed in a sand trap behind the green, and his third went past the hole by six feet. Woods two-putted for a par and then watched while Love's putt to tie slipped past the hole.

What most golfers take years to do and many never do—win a PGA Tour event—Tiger Woods had done in just his fifth try. His fellow pros were not surprised. "We all knew he was going to win some time," Love said. "I just didn't want it to be today."[13]

His victory at Las Vegas ran Woods's total earnings to $477,238. His status as a PGA Tour member was assured. Another goal was now in sight—a place in the season-ending Tour Championship, open only to the top thirty money winners.

A third-place tie at the La Cantera Texas Open the following week boosted Woods to thirty-fourth on the money list. He had one more chance to make the top thirty—the Walt Disney/Oldsmobile Classic. He opened the tournament with a 69, but that was six strokes behind the leaders. "Pop," he told his father that night, "I'm going to shoot 63 tomorrow and get back into this tournament."[14]

Sure enough, he shot a 63 on Friday and then another 69 on Saturday to pull within one shot of the lead. On Saturday night, he got a call from his mother. She told him to wear red on Sunday. Because he had been born in December, she said, red was his lucky color, according to a Thai tradition.

The next day, wearing a red shirt and a red hat, Tiger Woods shot a 66. He was tied at twenty-one under par with Taylor Smith, but when Smith was disqualified for using an illegal club, Woods was the winner. "I have some mixed feelings about it," Tiger said of his victory. "I feel like there should have been a playoff with Taylor."[15]

His winner's check for $216,000 put him into the Tour Championship, held at Southern Hills Golf Club in Tulsa, Oklahoma. He had a decent first-round score of 70, four shots off the lead. Early the next morning, however, his father was taken to a hospital with chest pains. He had suffered a heart attack.

Tiger Woods spent most of the night as his father's side. With his father in stable condition, Woods returned to the course on Friday, but he could not concentrate on his game, shooting a 78. "I just want to get done and go see my dad," he told playing partner John Cook.[16] Earl Woods recovered and within a few months was on the course, watching Tiger again.

He finished the tournament tied for twenty-first place. The 1996 PGA Tour schedule had come to an end. In just eight events, Tiger Woods had won $790,594—good enough for twenty-fourth on the money list. He had two victories and five top-ten finishes.

It was not enough for Tiger Woods, however. "I just want to be the best there is," he said.[17] For that, he would only have to wait one more year.

Chapter 8

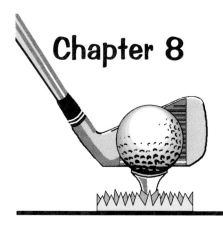

Year of the Tiger

They stood together on the seventh tee at La Costa Resort in California, peering through the rain at the green 188 yards away. A few nights earlier, they had been honored at the PGA Tour's annual awards banquet. Tom Lehman, leading money winner in 1996, had been named Player of the Year. Tiger Woods had been named the Tour's Rookie of the Year.

Now, on Sunday, January 12, 1997, they were tied after three rounds of the Mercedes Championships. A steady rain had washed out the final round, but one hole, the seventh, had been made ready for a playoff.

The hole was at the back left of the green,

FACT

When Tiger Woods won the 1996 Mercedes Championship in a play-off with Tom Lehman, he won $216,000. That win gave him total professional career earnings of $1,006,594. He had reached the $1 million mark in only nine tournaments—quicker than anyone in history. Ernie Els of South Africa held the old record, having become a millionaire after eighteen events.

dangerously close to a lake. Lehman would be hitting first. He pulled a 6 iron from his bag and stepped up to the ball. He swung and watched as the ball started for the green. Lehman twisted to the right, hoping somehow that the ball would straighten out. Instead, it splashed into the water.

All Woods had to do now was to play it safe and hit his tee shot safely to the middle of the green, take two putts for a par, and the championship would be his. Almost five thousand fans had stayed throughout the rain. They watched as Tiger Woods's ball sailed off the tee. It curved to the left. Would it, too, find the water?

The ball bit into the soggy green and rolled to a stop six inches from the hole. The crowd roared. Moments later, Woods tapped in the putt for the victory—his third in nine starts on the PGA Tour. His check for $216,000 put him over the $1 million mark for his short career. No other golfer had ever won $1 million so quickly.

Two weeks later, Woods stayed in contention at the Phoenix Open in Arizona, but with a fourth-round 72 he finished in a tie for ninth. Then it was on to California for the AT&T Pebble Beach National Pro-Am.

The final round at Pebble Beach came down to Tiger Woods and his good friend and Orlando neighbor Mark O'Meara. O'Meara had won at Pebble Beach four times. Woods made a late charge with birdies on sixteen and seventeen, but O'Meara was equal to the challenge with birdies on the same holes to stay one stroke ahead.

Down by one stroke, Woods knew he would probably have to score an eagle three on the final hole to win or tie. His second shot sailed 267 yards onto the green, and the crowd roared, expecting another miracle finish. His forty-foot putt just missed, however, and he had to settle for a 64 and second place. "I'm both disappointed and excited," he said afterward. "I had too little, too late."[1]

The runner-up spot, however, was good for $167,200. Tiger Woods now had won $403,450 in only three events. He had taken a lead in the race for the top money winner's position, which he would never lose.

He failed to mount any kind of challenge in his next three tournaments. He had one top-ten finish, ninth at Arnold Palmer's Bay Hill Invitational. But he ended up a distant thirty-first at The Players Championship a week later in Ponte Vedra Beach, Florida. For the first time in his professional career, he failed to shoot a round below 70 and also finished the 72 holes above par.

By most standards, Tiger Woods had had a good

year so far—one victory, 3 top-ten finishes—but he was far from satisfied. He took a week off to prepare for The Masters, working on his game with Harmon. On the Monday before the tournament, he showed that he was ready. Playing with O'Meara at Isleworth Country Club near Orlando, Woods set a course record with a thirteen-under-par 59.

Then it was off to Augusta and his amazing, record-setting Masters victory. In the space of four days, Tiger Woods had gone from just another star

Fan attendance at any tournament increases dramatically whenever Tiger Woods plays.

athlete to a national hero. President Bill Clinton called to invite Woods to a baseball game honoring Jackie Robinson, the first African American to play in the major leagues. Woods politely declined. He already had vacation plans. Oprah Winfrey had called, inviting him to be on her network television show, and he had accepted.

Woods took a month off the tour, returning for the GTE Byron Nelson Classic near Dallas, Texas. He promptly won again. This time, instead of being slow out of the gate, he fired a 64 in each of the first two rounds. He closed with a 67 and 68 but still broke the tournament record and won by two strokes.

Afterward, he told reporters he had not been at his best—that he had won with his "C-game" instead of his "A-game," as at The Masters. Some of his fellow golfers took offense. "He's making it sound like he's the only one," said Brad Faxon. "It's the mark of a champion to win tournaments without having everything together."[2] A week later, Tiger stopped grading his game in public.

At the MasterCard Colonial in Fort Worth, Texas, what was now being called Tigermania reached a fever pitch. Could Woods make it three tournaments in a row? Reporters and television networks came from all over the world. At Woods's Tuesday news

FACT

Tiger Woods once accidentally offended his colleagues. After his victory at The Masters, he found tournament programs and various items left by other pros in front of his locker with notes requesting autographs. He refused to take the time, not knowing that it was customary and that the items would go to charity auctions. He later complied with the autograph requests.

Woods stretches and limbers up before teeing off at the first hole of the 1997 MasterCard Colonial.

conference, he faced a lineup of twenty-two television cameras.

The strain of the past few weeks was starting to show. Woods was abrupt in his answers to reporters. He moved quickly through the crowds, shielded from autograph seekers by a squad of police and security personnel. When he took a two-shot lead after three rounds, the excitement grew. A mob of photographers recorded every shot. People screamed for autographs as he walked from hole to hole, something considered poor manners at golf tournaments.

A late double bogey dropped him into a tie for fourth place. Then Woods hurried into the locker room, instructing security men to keep reporters out, even though they are permitted in locker rooms by the PGA Tour. He changed clothes quickly and left to catch a plane.

The media was highly critical of Tiger's refusal to speak. One reporter wrote that "in a few short minutes, a guy who had become a media darling . . . looked like another prima donna and sore loser."[3]

Two weeks later, the spotlight was just as intense as Woods went to Congressional Country Club outside Washington, D.C., for the U.S. Open. Since he had won The Masters, the question was, could he win the Grand Slam—the four major tournaments all in one year? No golfer had done it. Jack Nicklaus had been the last, fifteen years earlier, to win even the first two.

It could be done, Woods said. Phil Mickelson had won four tournaments the year before. "They just have to be the right four," Tiger said.[4] Still, he said, winning the Grand Slam was not something he was thinking about. He might think about it if he won the first three and was leading in the last round of the fourth.

As the 1997 PGA Tour season wore on, Tiger Woods was the subject of ever-increasing attention from the news media.

Nevertheless, when he shot a four-over-par 74 on the first day, his disappointment showed. He rushed past reporters, through the locker room, and into the parking lot. Opening the door of his car, he slammed a portable CD player onto the floor. When asked what his thoughts were about his round, he said, "You don't want to know."[5]

He recovered nicely with a 67 on Friday, but with a 73–72 over the weekend he finished in a tie for nineteenth place. The Grand Slam dream was over—at least for another year.

The next week brought another disappointing finish, a tie for forty-third in the Buick Classic. People were beginning to say Tiger Woods could not take the pressure. He proved them wrong, winning the following week at the Western Open in Lemont, Illinois. He had now won four tournaments, and the PGA Tour season was barely half over. "If [Tiger] won three or four more, no one would be drastically surprised," said runner-up Frank Nobilo.[6]

The Western Open, however, would be Tiger Woods's last victory of 1997. He was well back in the other two major tournaments—twenty-fourth at the British Open and twenty-ninth at the PGA Championship. At the Canadian Open, he shot a 76 in the second round and failed to make the cut for the first time as a professional.

FACT

No golfer has ever won the modern "Grand Slam"—The Masters, British Open, U.S. Open, and PGA Championship— in the same year. In 1930, Bobby Jones won what was at that time considered the Grand Slam—the British and U.S. Opens and the British and U.S. Amateurs. Only one player—Ben Hogan in 1953—won as many as three in the same year, and only four players— Ben Hogan, Jack Nicklaus, Gary Player, and Gene Sarazen—have victories in all four tournaments sometime during the course of their careers.

It even seemed that the money title, which seemed a sure thing in July, might slip away. A victory in the season-ending Tour Championship by either Davis Love III or Justin Leonard might let them surpass Tiger Woods. For a time, that seemed likely. Late in the final round, Love took a two-shot lead. When Woods bogeyed the eighteenth hole to finish twelfth in the thirty-man field, he hurried away from the course, thinking he had lost the money title.

Love, however, made two bogeys down the stretch and dropped to third behind David Duval and Jim Furyk. Tiger Woods was the top money winner. His check for $97,600 pushed his 1997 total to $2,066,833, making him the first golfer ever to go over $2 million on the PGA Tour.

Still, it was a disappointing finish, and another disappointment was just ahead. Tiger Woods won only one of his five matches in the Ryder Cup competition between teams from the United States and Europe. When he was defeated in the singles match by Colin Montgomerie, it broke a string of thirty-seven match-play victories dating back to 1993.

When it was all over, Woods admitted that the hectic pace had gotten to him. "I definitely hit a wall right around the [U.S.] Open mentally, and physically toward the end of the year," he said. "Trying to understand everything that was happening in my life wore me out mentally."[7]

On his calendar for December 1997 was plenty of rest—and no golf. "I'm putting up the sticks [clubs] for a while, and it's going to be nice," he said. "It's been a long year. But it's been great."[8]

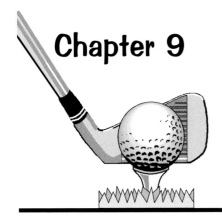

Chapter 9

Looking Back and Beyond

Once again, the finest golfers in the world gathered on the eve of the Mercedes Championships. At the previous year's awards banquet, Tiger Woods had been named Rookie of the Year. Now, on January 7, 1998, he was named Player of the Year. It was the first time anyone had won the award in just his first full year on the Tour.

"Earning their respect for your game is the most important part," Woods said. "I've made my presence known on the tour. I've proven myself to the other players."[1]

It was Woods's second major award in eight days. On December 31, he had been named Male Athlete of the Year for 1997 by the Associated Press.

He was only the fifth golfer ever to win the award and the first since Lee Trevino in 1971.

It had, indeed, been a good year and a very eventful one for Tiger Woods. Nothing would ever be the same—certainly for him, and possibly for the game of golf. When 1997 began, Tiger Woods was the best-known golfer in the world. When the year ended, he was perhaps the best-known personality in the world—in any walk of life.

Golf had had its superstars before, but the sport had never seen anything like the huge, frenzied crowds that followed Tiger Woods. Fans yelled for him to look their way, having brought cameras onto the golf course in violation of PGA Tour rules. They jostled one another to get in position for his autograph. Some wanted only to reach out and touch him. As the year went on, Woods was unable to move around the course without a squad of security officers to keep the fans at arm's length. The frenzy extended off the course, as well. Teenage girls once screamed his name so loudly outside his hotel that he finally had to come to the window and wave. "It was like he was the Pope," said his mother.[2]

Woods seemed at times to enjoy the attention, but as the year went on, it was clear that he was getting weary of the constant spotlight. He complained that he could not eat at a restaurant

FACT

Tigermania can sometimes border on the ridiculous. When Woods hit two shots into a pond at the Quad Cities Classic, an enterprising fan scooped up water from the pond into tiny bottles, which he then sold as souvenirs. At one tournament, after Tiger got a haircut in the clubhouse barber shop, fans clamored for locks of his hair.

without being hounded for autographs. "People want an autograph when you have food in your mouth," he said. "At the end of last year [1997] I didn't think it could get any worse, but you should never think that way. But once I won The Masters, yeah, my life did change."[3]

Although usually surrounded by people, he still felt lonely at times. He missed being just one of the guys in his Stanford dormitory. "I miss sitting around . . . and talking half the night," he said.

The center of attention wherever he goes, Tiger Woods is escorted through the course by security personnel.

"There's no one my own age to hang out with anymore because almost everyone my age is in college. . . . My mother was right when she said that turning pro would take away my youth."[4]

The only place he could truly be his own person was on the golf course, using his immense powers of concentration to block out the crowds of people surrounding him. "No one can get to me out there," he said.[5]

Turning pro might have taken Woods's privacy, but it also gave him tremendous wealth. The $2 million he won during 1997 was just the beginning. In addition to the deals with Nike and Titleist, Woods also signed agreements with All-Star Cafe restaurants, the American Express credit card company, and Rolex watches. *Forbes* magazine estimated his total income for the year at $26.1 million, making him the sixth-highest-paid professional athlete in the United States.

Unlike many other sports stars, Tiger Woods takes an active interest in his business deals. He formed his own corporation, ETW (Eldrick Tiger Woods). He takes part in all the major marketing decisions. "This is my life, and anything that involves my time, I want to have a say-so," he said. "Other people making decisions for me—if they think that's for me, then we're going to have a clash."[6]

Tiger Woods's fame has brought financial benefits to the game of golf as well as to Woods, himself. The Associated Press, after interviewing tournament officials and executives of television networks and golf equipment companies, estimated that Woods brought an additional $653.5 million into golf.

Much of the increase was in television revenue. The four major tournaments were watched in an estimated 19 million households in 1996. In 1997, the figure leaped to more than 30 million. The PGA Tour was able to take advantage of the jump in ratings to negotiate a four-year television deal of $650 million, an increase of $325 million.

Not only were more people watching golf on television, they were also flocking to see tournaments. Ticket sales increased dramatically, particularly when Tiger Woods was playing. Attendance at the B.C. Open, for instance, rose by 35 percent, and concession and souvenir sales were up 28 percent. "We had to cut off ticket sales about a week before the tournament," said Mac Wesson of the Byron Nelson Classic, "because we thought we'd be unable to serve the people who were there."[7]

The Tiger Woods phenomenon had a negative

effect, however, on the tournaments he chose not to play. The thousands of newcomers—those who came to tournaments and those who watched on television—wanted first of all to see Tiger Woods. Golf was secondary. People began to have the idea that a tournament without Tiger Woods was not worth watching. It was no wonder that when Woods promised to play in the Disney Classic, the tournament director jumped fully clothed into a swimming pool to celebrate.

More people were playing golf, as well. Sales of golf equipment increased $5 billion in 1997. Course fees and cart rentals increased $10 billion. Nike's sales of golf clothing and shoes doubled to $120 million.

Most of the newcomers would not have given golf a second thought had it not been for Tiger Woods. What had been a game primarily for upper-middle-class whites began to spread to all segments of society. John Morrison, director of an urban golf program in Los Angeles, said, "I think Tiger has been able to do what very few golfers have been able to do in the past—he made golf 'cool.'"[8]

What exactly is Tiger Woods's appeal? What, in addition to his tremendous talent, has made him so attractive? "First of all," said his teacher, Butch Harmon, "he's still a kid. People love that, to see a

FACT

Tiger Woods was not the first golfer to win $2 million in a single year. Woods won $2,066,833 to lead the regular PGA Tour. Just a few weeks earlier, however, Hale Irwin had topped the $2 million mark in the PGA Senior Tour. In that series of tournaments, open to players over the age of fifty, Irwin won $2,343,365 for the year.

younger person succeed in a man's world, so to speak. And that smile. You've got to love it."[9]

People are also attracted by the tremendous power Tiger Woods displays. The thrill of seeing him drive a golf ball 325 yards is much the same as seeing a long home run in baseball or a 100 mile-per-hour serve in tennis. Then, too, there's Woods's obvious intensity and burning desire. "He wants to win every time out," said advertising executive Richard Zien. "He wants to make his opponents fear him. The crowd feels that; they're drawn to that pure aggression."[10]

Part of Tiger Woods's appeal is based on his mixed heritage. Tournament crowds, once almost all-white, are liberally sprinkled with African Americans when Woods is playing. More African-American young people are taking up golf instead of basketball or baseball. Tiger Woods is doing his part by creating a foundation to provide golf equipment and lessons to inner-city kids.

Woods is not entirely comfortable with being labeled a black golfer. "I'm not out to be the best black player," he said. "I want to be the best golfer ever."[11] He knows, however, that such labels are inevitable. "Unfortunately, that's the way our society is right now," he said. "We can't look at a person and say we're part of the same race, the human race."[12]

As a result, Tiger Woods is willing to be a symbol for African Americans. He is also willing to be a role model, something many professional athletes try to avoid. "I like the idea of being a role model," he said. "It's an honor. People took time to help me as a kid, and they impacted my life. I want to do the same for kids."[13]

Watching Tiger Woods play is not always easy. Sometimes the fans are stacked ten-deep around the tees, making it hard to see anything.

Woods's father, for one, thinks his son's influence will go far, far beyond the game of golf. "He will transcend this game and bring to the world a humanitarianism which has never been known before," Earl Woods said. "The world will be a better place to live in by virtue of his existence and his presence. . . . He can hold everyone together. He is the Universal Child."[14]

Tiger Woods does not go quite that far, but he does think that everyone and everything has a purpose. "I feel that everything that happens happens for a reason," he said. "And I feel that the person upstairs puts each person on this planet and gives them a limit of things they can handle. And that person up there feels that I can handle a lot so then He gives me a lot."[15]

What lies ahead for Tiger Woods? How good can he be? What must be frightening for his fellow professionals is that Tiger Woods's game—as good as it is—is still getting better. His short game—the delicate shots around the green—improved during 1997, as did his putting. "He is a golf machine," said fellow pro Woody Austin. "He is so mentally tough, so physically gifted. There are no kinks in the armor."[16]

At the age of twenty-one, Tiger Woods climbed to the top of a sport usually dominated by men in their thirties. Some people wondered if it was too much success too soon. "You can't know today how the wealth will affect his passion for golf tomorrow," said television commentator Frank Hannigan.[17]

The money, Woods says, is not that important. "I can enjoy material things, but that doesn't mean I need them." he said. "I'd be fine in a shack, as long as I could play some golf."[18] What matters most to Tiger Woods is not money, but winning. "I expect to win every tournament that I play because that's what I go there to do," he said.[19]

Whatever Tiger Woods accomplishes in golf will never be enough—for Tiger Woods. He may set all sorts of records, but then he will try just as hard to break his own records. It is that inner fire, said sports psychologist Jay Brunza, who knows Tiger better than anyone else except his parents, that will keep him going. "This kid is not going to burn out," Brunza said. "He's not going to be a shooting star because he's playing the game for the joy and passion within himself."[20]

As for Tiger Woods, the future will take care of itself. He is too busy enjoying the present. When a reporter asked him if he was having fun, he replied, "I'm having the time of my life."[21]

Woods continued to play great golf in 1998, but the victories did not come at the same pace. He had four top-ten finishes in the first four tournaments he played, but it was not until May 10, 1998, that he broke what was—for him—a victory drought by winning the BellSouth Classic in Atlanta, Georgia.

Going into the 1998 Tour Championship in late October, Woods had posted ten top-ten finishes and had won more than $1.5 million. He had not yet come to dominate the sport, as many had predicted he would, but—at age twenty-three—there was still plenty of time.

Chapter Notes

Chapter 1. The Youngest Master

1. Jimmy Burch, "Driving Toward a Title," *Fort Worth Star-Telegram*, April 12, 1997, p. D11.

2. "Woods Opens Whopping Nine-Shot Lead Entering Sunday's Final Round of The Masters," <www.pgatour.com> (April 12, 1997).

3. CBS Television Network broadcast of the Masters Tournament, April 12, 1997.

4. Larry Dorman, "Woods's 65 Leaves Field Far Back and Masters Record Near," *The New York Times*, April 13, 1997, p. B19.

5. Jimmy Burch, "A Tiger Q&A," *Fort Worth Star-Telegram*, May 18, 1997, p. K4.

6. *Oprah Winfrey Show*, ABC Television Network broadcast, April 25, 1997.

7. CBS Television Network broadcast The Masters golf tournament, April 13, 1997.

8. "Tiger Woods Takes Historic, Record-Setting Victory at The Masters," <www.pgatour.com> (April 13, 1997).

9. Jimmy Burch, "GRRREATT!," *Fort Worth Star-Telegram*, April 14, 1997, p. C13.

10. Frank Luksa, "Mind of a Champion Doesn't Permit Failure," *The Dallas Morning News*, April 12, 1997, p. B8.

11. Brad Townsend, "Woods Shows Masters Touch," *Dallas Morning News*, April 14, 1997, p. A8.

12. *Oprah Winfrey Show*, ABC Television Network broadcast, April 25, 1997.

Chapter 2. Golf—A Brief Description

No notes.

Chapter 3. The Cub

1. Earl Woods, *Training a Tiger* (New York: HarperCollins Publishers, 1997), p. xviii.

2. John Strege, *Tiger: A Biography of Tiger Woods* (New York: Broadway Books, 1997), p. 11.

3. Ibid.

4. Tim Rosaforte, *Tiger Woods: The Makings of a Champion* (New York: St. Martin's Press, 1997), p. 16.

5. Strege, p. 12.

6. Woods, p. x.

7. Bill Gutman, *Tiger Woods: A Biography* (New York: Archway Paperback, 1997), p. 21.

8. *Oprah Winfrey Show*, ABC Television Network broadcast, April 25, 1997.

9. Strege, p. 21.

10. Woods, p. 13.

11. Gutman, p. 18.

12. Strege, p. 22.

Chapter 4. Child Prodigy

1. John Strege, *Tiger: A Biography of Tiger Woods* (New York: Broadway Books, 1997), p. 26.

2. Ibid., p. 34.

3. Tim Rosaforte, *Tiger Woods: The Makings of a Champion* (New York: St. Martin's Press, 1997), p. 22.

4. Earl Woods, *Training a Tiger* (New York: HarperCollins Publishers, 1997), p. 149.

5. Ibid.

6. S. A. Kramer, *Tiger Woods: Golfing to Greatness* (New York: Random House, 1997), p. 15.

7. Rosaforte, p. 25.

8. Ibid., p. 27.

9. Strege, p. 29.

10. Rosaforte, p. 22.

11. Bill Gutman, *Tiger Woods: A Biography* (New York: Archway Paperback, 1997), p. 29.

12. Strege, p. 37.

13. Gutman, p. 31.

14. Rosaforte, p. 40.

Chapter 5. The Legend Grows

1. Tim Rosaforte, *Tiger Woods: The Makings of a Champion* (New York: St. Martin's Press, 1997), p. 43.

2. John Garrity, "You the Kid!" *Tiger Woods: The Making of a Champion* (New York: Simon & Schuster, 1996), p. 18.

3. Rosaforte, p. 67.

4. John Strege, *Tiger: A Biography of Tiger Woods* (New York: Broadway Books, 1997), p. 57.

5. Rosaforte, p. 66.

6. Ibid., p. 72.

7. Tim Crowthers, "No Holding This Tiger," *Tiger Woods: The Making of a Champion* (New York: Simon & Schuster, 1996), p. 20.

8. Strege, p. 147.

9. Ibid., p. 74.

10. Rosaforte, p. 95.

11. S.A. Kramer, *Tiger Woods: Golfing to Greatness* (New York: Random House, 1997), p. 52.

12. Crowthers, p. 25.

Chapter 6. Student and Superstar

1. Tim Rosaforte, *Tiger Woods: The Makings of a Champion* (New York: St. Martin's Press, 1997), p. 83.

2. Mark Soltau, "Natural Born Thriller," Becket Profiles (Dallas, Tex.: Statabase, Inc., 1997), p. 27.

3. John Strege, *Tiger: A Biography of Tiger Woods* (New York: Broadway Books, 1997), p. 102.

4. Rosaforte, p. 125.

5. Jamie Diaz, "Out of Sight," *Tiger Woods: The Making of a Champion* (New York: Simon & Schuster, 1996), p. 44.

6. Bill Gutman, *Tiger Woods: A Biography* (New York: Archway Paperback, 1997), p. 41.

7. Strege, p. 134.

8. Rosaforte, p. 130.

9. Ibid., p. 151.

10. Gutman, p. 48.

11. Strege, p. 142.

12. Ibid., p. 2.

13. Gutman, p. 53.

14. Rosaforte, p. 169.

Chapter 7. Professional Golfer

1. S.A. Kramer, *Tiger Woods: Golfing to Greatness* (New York: Random House, 1997), p. 78.

2. Tim Rosaforte, *Tiger Woods: The Makings of a Champion* (New York: St. Martin's Press, 1997), p. 31.

3. Phil Rogers, "Forecast: Reign," Becket Profiles (Dallas, Tex.: Statabase, Inc., 1997), p. 60.

4. Rosaforte, p. 176.

5. John Strege, *Tiger: A Biography of Tiger Woods* (New York: Broadway Books, 1997), p. 197.

6. Interview at Media Center, Congressional Country Club, Bethesda, Md., June 10, 1997.

7. "He's BAAACK," <www.pgatour.com> (January 8, 1997).

8. Strege, p. 202.

9. Rosaforte, p. 199.

10. Gary Smith, "The Chosen One," *Sports Illustrated*, December 23, 1996, p. 41.

11. Rosaforte, p. 203.

12. Strege, p. 210.

13. Thomas Bonk, "I Am Tiger Woods," Becket Profiles (Dallas, Tex.: Statabase, Inc., 1997), p. 12.

14. Strege, p. 215.

15. Ibid., p. 216.

16. Rosaforte, p. 234.

17. Bonk, p. 12.

Chapter 8. Year of the Tiger

1. "Mark O'Meara Captures Fifth AT&T Pebble Beach National Pro-Am Title," <www.pgatour.com> (January 15, 1997).

2. Ron Sirak, "Tiger Deserves an A for His First Year as a Pro," Associated Press electronic release, August 27, 1997.

3. Kevin Blackistone, "Tiger's Silence Brings End to Honeymoon With Media," *The Dallas Morning News*, May 28, 1997, p. B2.

4. Interview at Media Center, Congressional Country Club, Bethesda, Md., June 10, 1997.

5. Author interview, Congressional Country Club, Bethesda, Md., June 12, 1997.

6. "Tiger Woods Makes the Motorola Western Open His Fourth Victory of 1997," <www.pgatour.com> (July 6, 1997).

7. Ron Sirak, "Woods Waxes About the Future," Associated Press electronic release, December 11, 1997.

8. Jimmy Burch, "The Year of the Tiger," *Fort Worth Star-Telegram*, November 2, 1997, p C20.

Chapter 9. Looking Back and Beyond

1. Associated Press, "Woods, Palmer Honored by PGA Tour," *The New York Times*, <www.nytimes.com> January 10, 1998.

2. Phil Rogers, "Forecast: Reign," *Becket Profiles* (Dallas, Tex.: Statabase, Inc., 1997), p. 62.

3. Interview at Media Center, Congressional Country Club, Bethesda, Md., June 10, 1997.

4. Gary Smith, "The Chosen One," *Sports Illustrated*, December 23, 1996, p. 37.

5. Ron Sirak, "Woods Waxes About the Future," Associated Press electronic release, December 11, 1997.

6. Ron Stodghill II, "Tiger, Inc.," *Business Week*, April 28, 1997, p. 34.

7. Ron Sirak, "The Tiger Industry Keeps Growing," Associated Press electronic release, August 27, 1997.

8. Stodghill, p. 36.

9. Thomas Bonk, "I Am Tiger Woods," *Becket Profiles* (Dallas, Tex.: Statabase, Inc., 1997), p. 10.

10. Stodghill, p. 34.

11. Gary D'Amato, "Major Talent," *Becket Profiles* (Dallas, Tex.: Statabase, Inc., 1997), p. 46.

12. Interview at Media Center, Congressional Country Club, Bethesda, Md., June 10, 1997.

13. Smith, p. 44.

14. Ibid., p. 31.

15. Interview, June 10, 1997.

16. Woody Austin, "Woody's Take on Tiger," <http://www.golfweb.com/library/austin/austin970704.html> (July 4, 1997).

17. "Tiger: How He's Changing Your Game," *Golf Digest*, Vol. 48, No. 7, July 1997, p. 83.

18. Smith, p. 49.

19. Interview, June 10, 1997.

20. Phil Rogers, "A League of His Own," *Becket Profiles* (Dallas, Tex.: Statabase, Inc., 1997), p. 57.

21. Andy Brumer, "Year of the Tiger," *Petersen's Golfing*, January 1997, p. 23.

Tournament Statistics

(in chronological order)

1996			
Tournament	**+/- Par**	**Place**	**Earnings**
Greater Milwaukee Open	-7	Tied for 60th	$2,544
Canadian Open	-8	Tied for 11th	$37,500
Quad Cities Classic	-10	Tied for 5th	$42,150
B.C. Open	-16	Tied for 3rd	$58,000
Las Vegas Invitational	-28	1st	$297,000
La Cantera Texas Open	-11	3rd	$81,600
Walt Disney World/Oldsmobile Classic	-21	1st	$216,000
Tour Championship	+8	Tied for 21st	$55,800
Total			**$790,594**

1997			
Tournament	+/- Par	Place	Earnings
Mercedes Championship	-14	1st	$216,000
Phoenix Open	-9	Tied for 18th	$20,250
AT&T Pebble Beach National Pro-Am	-19	Tied for 2nd	$167,200
Nissan Open	-3	Tied for 20th	$14,600
Bay Hill Invitational	-10	Tied for 9th	$42,000
The Players Championship	+1	Tied for 31st	$20,300
The Masters Tournament	-18	1st	$486,000
GTE Byron Nelson Classic	-17	1st	$324,000
MasterCard Colonial	-12	Tied for 4th	$70,000
Memorial Tournament	+5	Tied for 67th	$3,800
U.S. Open	+6	Tied for 19th	$31,916
Buick Classic	+3	Tied for 43rd	$4,568
Motorola Western Open	-13	1st	$360,000
British Open	Even	Tied for 24th	$17,362
Buick Open	-10	Tied for 8th	$43,500
PGA Championship	+6	Tied for 29th	$13,625
NEC World Series of Golf	-2	Tied for 3rd	$114,000
Bell Canadian Open	+6	Cut	N/A
Walt Disney World/Oldsmobile Classic	-10	Tied for 26th	$10,650
Las Vegas Invitational	-5	Tied for 36th	$8,663
Tour Championship	-3	Tied for 12th	$97,600
Total			**$2,066,034**

1998			
Tournament	**+/- Par**	**Place**	**Earnings**
Mercedes Championship	-16	Tied for 2nd	$149,600
AT&T Pebble Beach National Pro-Am	+4	Cut	N/A
Buick Invitational	-11	Tied for 3rd	$109,200
Nissan Open	-12	2nd	$226,800
Doral-Ryder Open	-5	Tied for 9th	$48,000
Bay Hill Invitational	-4	Tied for 13th	$37,500
Players Championship	+2	Tied for 35th	$18,885
The Masters Tournament	-3	Tied for 8th	$89,600
BellSouth Classic	-17	1st	$324,000
GTE Byron Nelson Classic	-8	Tied for 12th	$52,500
Memorial Tournament	Even	Tied for 51st	$5,148
U.S. Open	+10	Tied for 18th	$41,833
Motorola Western Open	-7	Tied for 9th	$49,225
British Open	+1	3rd	$222,075
Buick Open	-13	Tied for 4th	$96,000
Sprint International*	N/A	4th	$96,000
NEC World Series of Golf	-5	Tied for 5th	$85,500
Total (through October 14)			**$1,651,866**

*Sprint International uses a point system rather than standing relative to par.

Where to Write
Tiger Woods

Mr. Tiger Woods
c/o IMG Center
Suite 100
1360 E. 9th Street
Cleveland, OH 44114

On the Internet at:
Tiger Woods Home Page
<http://www.sonic.net/~lindab/>

Tiger Woods Fan Page
<http://www.nicom.com/~sports/tiger/woods.htm>

Tiger Woods Chat Room
<http://www.golfsw.com/tiger.htm>

Index